Parenting With a Purpose

A 31-Day Devotional

By Karen Jensen Salisbury

All scripture taken from the *New King James Version* of the
Bible unless otherwise noted

Karen Jensen Salisbury

INTRODUCTION

To Parents:

First, let me say: hurray for you for picking up this devotional! It means you want to raise your children "in the discipline and instruction of the Lord" (Ephesians 6:4 ESV). There is no greater legacy to leave to your children – good for you!

Second, as you read through it, I want you to know that God is on your side. He believes the best for you and your family. Parenting can be the most delightful, frustrating, exhilarating, confusing, exciting, exhausting job on the planet! But God knew what He was doing when He made you a parent, and when He put your child(ren) in your family – you have all His grace and power and love backing you.

This book contains verses and declarations that I used when my children were growing up. When they were 12 & 13 years old, their father (my first husband) died very suddenly, and I didn't remarry until they were grown and married themselves. So I have been a married parent and a single parent, and I can testify to the fact that no matter what your circumstances are,

God is faithful! He has seen us through in every situation. Both my sons are still serving God with all their hearts today, raising their own kids, and I can tell you with certainty: God's Word works. And I still use this devotional to speak God's Word over them – because we never stop being the parent.

But back to their childhood… back then I wrote these verses and declarations down because there were some days I couldn't think of one scripture on my own to use to keep them surrounded with faith! On those days of trouble or crisis or bewilderment, I would grab my notebook like a lifeline and begin to read the very words you're about to read, saying to myself, "Oh yes that's right, this is what I believe! Thank you Lord for helping me get back into faith in this situation."

This is a tool to help you plant the Word in your heart and mind, and the hearts and minds of your children. Its purpose is two-fold:

1)   To give you, as a parent, God's vision for your children. To help you every day to see them the way He does – as a blessing and a joy, a responsibility and a delight, with

unlimited potential and a God-given destiny. To release faith, protection, love and power into your child's life by consistently speaking God's Word over them.

2)   To give your child a vision for their life from the Word of God. To help them speak the Word – to say what God says about them – which will empower them to understand who they are as children of God.

You can use this book in many different ways. You can use it as a family devotional, reading it together with your kids in the morning or at night before bed. You can have them read it to you in the car on the way to school (or wherever). You can read it by yourself, or your children can read it by themselves. You can look up the scriptures in your own Bible and highlight them, or just read them from here. You can read each entry one day at a time over the period of a year, starting over at the beginning of every month, or you can use it whenever you need some parental encouragement, reading as many days as you want! (There were days I read through the whole thing…)

Put the name of your child or children in the place where it says "my children." Meditate on the truth from God's Word about your child all day long. Remember, we are confessing what we want over our children, based on Romans 4:17, not what we have!

Happy parenting! Enjoy every moment...

Karen Jensen Salisbury

TABLE OF CONTENTS

Day One..........................God Has a Good Plan

Day Two.........................No Fear!

Day Three.......................The Holy Spirit Lives in Us

Day Four........................Godly Influences

Day Five.........................Wisdom and Favor

Day Six..........................Practicing Love

Day Seven......................Discovering our Purpose

Day Eight.......................Making Right Decisions

Day Nine........................We Have the Mind of Christ

Day Ten.........................Peace

Day Eleven.....................No Laziness Here!

Day Twelve....................Mighty Champions

Day Thirteen...................We Are Safe

Day Fourteen..................Correction Brings Wisdom

Day Fifteen.....................Enjoy the Teenage Years

Day Sixteen....................Our Family's Gift to the World

Day Seventeen.................Be Increase-Minded

Day Eighteen...................Send Them into All the World

Day Nineteen..................Be Kind and Forgive

Day Twenty...................Living By the Word

Day Twenty One...............Praying For Their Future Spouse

Day Twenty Two..............Good Friend, Good Spouse

Day Twenty Three.............God's Top Priority

TABLE OF CONTENTS (Con't)

Day Twenty Four.................A Work in Progress

Day Twenty Five..................Think About What You're Thinking About

Day Twenty Six...................Obedience Brings Blessing

Day Twenty Seven..............Raising God's Last Days Army

Day Twenty Eight...............Living Well for the Master

Day Twenty Nine................The Blood of Jesus

Day Thirty........................Refuse to Worry

Day Thirty One..................When They're Hurting

DAY ONE

God Has a Good Plan

"For I know the thoughts and plans I have for you, says the Lord, thoughts and plans for welfare and peace and not for evil, to give you hope in your final outcome."

Jeremiah 29:11 Amp.

Today's Meditation:

Whatever is happening today in the life of your family, there's good news – God has a plan. And it's a good plan! A plan for the welfare, peace, and hope of every member of your family. Your Heavenly Father is not surprised by where you find yourself today, and He's not worried either. He expects everything to turn out well. He can see the end from the beginning and He sees the final outcome as good. Time for you to start seeing it that way too.

Parent Declaration:

God has a wonderful, divinely ordered plan for my children's whole life. They have a divine destiny, and I proclaim that they are walking in it today. They are fulfilling

God's plan for their life, and they have a bright future.

Kid Declaration:

My future is bright! God has a good plan for me! □

DAY TWO

No Fear!

"God has not given us the spirit of fear; but of power, and of love, and of a sound mind."

2 Timothy 1:7

Today's Meditation:

There are plenty of reasons to fear for your children in today's world: there's the possibility of sickness and disease, drugs, gangs, bullies, kidnapping, internet pornography, or any number of horrors on the nightly news. But! God knew all about what raising a child today would look like, and He has empowered you to do it. And He has empowered your children. He hasn't given you a spirit of fear, but a spirit of power, and of love, and of a sound mind. Think about that today, and don't be afraid!

Parent Declaration:

I refuse to fear over my children. I surround them with faith and with the love of God. I imagine them successful, happy, protected and healthy. Whenever I think of my children and their future, I have a sound mind. I picture them surrounded with God's power and love.

Kid Declaration:

I'm not afraid today! God has given me the spirit of power, love, and a sound mind!☐

Resource: *For more help resisting fear, check out my* CD *or* MP3 *"Let Not Your Heart Be Troubled"*

DAY THREE

The Holy Spirit Lives in Us

"When the Spirit of truth has come, he will guide you into all truth...he shall teach you all things, and bring all things to your remembrance, whatever I have said to you."

John 16:13, 14:26

Today's Meditation:

As Christians, we have the Holy Spirit of God living right inside us. That gives us such an advantage! We have access to all His wisdom, His power, His joy, His peace, and His ability. That's true for you as a parent, and it's true for your child. Remind them every day that we are not living life in our own strength – we are overcomers because of the Greater One inside us (1 John 4:4). The Holy Spirit is guiding us, teaching us, and bringing things to our remembrance. He's helping us, all day long, in every way that we need Him.

Parent Declaration:

I trust the Greater One in my children today. He is leading them and guiding them into truth, and they listen to

His voice. He is teaching them and helping them whenever they need help. My faith is not in my children's ability to do everything right, but in the mighty Holy Spirit who lives in them. They are overcomers!

Kid Declaration:

God's Holy Spirit lives in me! He goes everywhere with me and is helping me to be an overcomer all day long. □

Resource: *To learn more about the Holy Spirit's power in your life check out my* CD *or* MP3 *called "ABCs of the Holy Spirit."*

DAY FOUR

Godly Influences

"Don't be unequally yoked together with unbelievers...Blessed is the man who walks not in the counsel of the ungodly, nor stands in the path of sinners, nor sits in the seat of the scornful."

2 Cor. 6:14, Ps. 1:1

Today's Meditation:

When my children were growing up I prayed what I like to call "the Teflon prayer" over them. There are all sorts of influences out there in the world, but we as parents can ask God to bring the good ones across our children's path, and not let any of the ungodly ones "stick" to them. Just as sticky foods slide right off Teflon, let's believe that our children will choose right friends, and that bad influences will slide right off them.

Parent Declaration:

Father, let no ungodly influence or friendship stick to my children. I say that every relationship not ordained of God in their lives would fizzle and disappear. They will not be unequally yoked in any way. Bring people into their lives to help and influence them for good, to infuse them with godly confidence and character.

Kid Declaration:

Father, thank You for bringing me good friends who will help me to know and obey You, all the days of my life.

Take Action: *Pray the "Teflon prayer" over your children each time they leave the house.*

DAY FIVE

Wisdom and Favor

"And Jesus increased in wisdom and stature, and in favor with God and man."

Luke 2:52

Today's Meditation:

This verse in the Bible was written about Jesus as a child. Our children can also increase in wisdom and in favor with God and man, *today*. They are a work in progress, and we can keep them surrounded with our faith and love, not with fear and doubt. Believe in the person they are becoming, and in the favor of God that surrounds them.

Parent Declaration:

Because I raise my children to follow Jesus, I declare that they have supernatural favor with God and man. As they grow up physically, they're also growing in wisdom and favor. They will have blessing and opportunities that others don't. The favor of God is upon them and people want to bless and help them. They are treated like sons of the Most High God everywhere they go.

Kid Declaration:

I am growing in wisdom and stature, and I have favor today with God and every person I meet.

DAY SIX

Practice Love

"Love endures with patience and serenity, love is kind and thoughtful, and is not jealous or envious...Love bears all things [regardless of what comes], believes all things [looking for the best in each one], hopes all things [remaining steadfast during difficult times], endures all things [without weakening]. Love never fails...."

1 Cor. 13:4-8 (AMP)

Today's Meditation:

The real test of spiritual maturity is not how much Bible we read, how many scriptures we memorize, or how often we go to church – the real test is walking in love with people. And families are where we practice! Make love the priority in your home, and you'll see God's presence and help every day among your loved ones. When we parents make a conscious effort to walk in love with our children, we teach them the greatest lesson of Christianity.

Parent Declaration:

My relationship with my children is blessed; we walk in love with each other and enjoy each other as God intended. Because we are all His children, and we obey Him and seek His will, His love is free to reign in our household. I bind strife and division between me and any family member, and I loose peace and harmony between us. Give us wisdom to bless and help each other. I declare that the enemy is not allowed to cause strife in our family in any way, shape or form.

Kid Declaration:

Today I will walk in love with my family and with other people – I will help and bless them.

Take Action: In our family we made great progress learning this great lesson when we wrote out 1 Corinthians 13:4-8 in the Amplified Bible – then we posted it on bathroom mirrors and read it every night at dinner. Try it at your house!

DAY SEVEN

Discovering Our Purpose

"...may (God) give to you the spirit of wisdom and revelation in the knowledge of Him, the eyes of your understanding being enlightened; that you may know what is the hope of His calling, what are the riches of the glory of His inheritance in the saints."

Ephesians 1:17, 18

Today's Meditation:

God has a purpose for every life, and that includes your children. What a great benefit it is for them to learn of His purpose – the hope of His calling – early on in their lives! We can create an environment for them to be sensitive to His voice and spiritually discern His plan for their lives. Instead of asking them, "What do you want to be when you grow up," help them focus in on, "What does *God* want me to be?" When they have God's wisdom and understanding, they are well on their way to living for Him, so let's speak that over them today.

Parent Declaration:

My children are hungry for the things of God. I declare that they have the spirit of wisdom working in their lives. They are seeking Him as to His plan for their life, and receiving insight into their divine destiny. Revelation from God flows to them – they see and understand spiritual things, and they know what God has called them to.

Kid Declaration:

I am learning and growing in God today! I am seeking Him to find out His good plan for me.

DAY EIGHT

Making Right Decisions

"I call heaven and earth as witnesses today against you, that I have set before you life and death, blessing and cursing; therefore choose life, that both you and your descendants may live."

Deuteronomy 30:19

Today's Meditation:

As parents, our main goal is to raise our children into adults who make right decisions for their own lives. When they're young, we make many decisions for them, but as they head into their teenage years, they begin the separation process. Eventually they will make their own decisions, and it's never too early to start helping them. When facing a decision, I used to ask my children, "What does your spirit man say?" I wanted them to start listening to the Guide on the Inside. Start believing today that your children will choose life (God's will) in every instance and make right decisions for themselves.

Parent Declaration:

My children make right choices for their lives. They make godly choices every day. They choose God's way to life: right friends, right decisions, right actions, and right thoughts. The blessing of God is upon them, and they are led by His Spirit in their choices.

Kid Declaration:

I will ask God for help today, and I will choose to make right decisions that please Him.

Resource: For more, check out my CD called "Helping Your Children Make Right Decisions"

DAY NINE

The Mind of Christ

"…we have the mind of Christ."

1 Corinthians 2:16

Today's Meditation:

When my children were school age, I sent them off every morning with this verse ringing in their ears and told them: "Remember, you have the mind of Christ and you are sharp learners today!" I also told them that because they listened and obeyed God, they were 10 times smarter than all the wise guys in the school – just like Shadrach, Meshach, Abednego, and Daniel were 10 times smarter than all the wise guys in the kingdom (Daniel 1:17-20). The mind of Christ is given to us through the Spirit of God (vv. 10-12) and it involves wisdom from God. Claim it by faith for your children and speak it over them daily!

Parent Declaration:

My children have the mind of Christ and they are sharp, life-long learners. I declare that they love to learn! They listen and obey the wisdom and direction of God today, and are 10 times smarter than those who don't. The Spirit of God helps them to understand and remember everything they learn.

Kid Declaration:

I have the mind of Christ, and as I listen and obey God, I am 10 times smarter than anyone who doesn't!

DAY TEN

Peace

"Your children shall be taught of the Lord; and great shall be the peace of your children."

Isaiah 54:13

Today's Meditation:

In today's world, with trouble and turmoil all around us, many people wish they had peace. Thankfully, the Bible says that when we teach our children about the Lord as they are growing up, we are bringing His peace into their lives. What a wonderful promise! In Hebrew the word for peace is *shalom,* which is translated "wholeness; nothing missing, nothing broken." Children who are taught of the Lord have wholeness in every area of their life, and that is a precious gift indeed.

Parent Declaration:

Because my children are taught of You, Lord, I declare that they have Your peace upon them in every sense of the word – wholeness, completeness, nothing lacking, nothing lost. That peace guides them and keeps them safe in the midst of any trial. My children have *great* peace in their lives.

Kid Declaration:

I'm taught of the Lord, so I have great peace!

DAY ELEVEN

No Laziness Here!

"He who has a slack hand becomes poor, but the hand of the diligent makes rich."

Proverbs 10:4

Today's Meditation:

Children are not born diligent – it's taught to them. Diligence is defined as "steady, earnest, and energetic effort." And the Bible promises good things to those who are diligent, not lazy. As parents, we want to do our part in teaching diligence to our children. One of the best ways to do that is by giving them chores and training them to be an active, working part of a household. If we do everything for our children or give them everything they want, they'll grow up ungrateful, demanding, and entitled. As we help them to become diligent at home, they will carry this skill throughout life and God promises that will make them rich.

Parent Declaration:

I speak over my children that they are diligent. They

are not lazy but good workers who persevere, even when it's hard. They stick with things and refuse to quit. They are steady, earnest and energetic. Because of that, they will not be poor but rich, according to God's Word.

Kid Declaration:

I am a diligent worker today – I'm not lazy!

Take action: *If you haven't already, assign chores to your children. For help, read my blog* "Kids and Chores."

DAY TWELVE

Mighty Champions

"Blessed is the man who fears the LORD, who delights greatly in His commandments. His descendants will be mighty on earth; the generation of the upright will be blessed."

Psalm 112:1, 2

Today's Meditation:

When we live our lives to please the Lord – when we put Him first, honor Him, delight in His Word – this is fearing the Lord. And He promises that it will carry down to our children, so that they will be "mighty on the earth." No matter what we see all around us every day, or how dark the future of the world looks, God says our children's generation shall be *blessed!* Let's stay in agreement with His promises and declare this over our children.

Parent Declaration:

Our family fears the Lord and delights in His Word. Therefore, my children shall be mighty on this earth – they shall be strong, they shall be champions, they shall always triumph. The hand of God is upon them, and they are blessed.

Kid Declaration:

God's hand is upon me and I am a mighty champion! My generation is blessed!

DAY THIRTEEN

We Are Safe

*"No evil shall befall you, nor shall any plague come near your dwelling;
for He shall give His angels charge over you, to keep you in all your
ways."*

Psalm 91:10, 11

Today's Meditation:

This verse almost seems too good to be true – but it *is*
true! We can claim it for our family. The entire chapter of
Psalm 91 is God's promise to protect us. If you've been
afraid over your children, spend more time reading this
encouraging chapter. Then instead of imagining the worst
happening, start imagining the angels that surround your
family, keeping you safe, warding off evil and disease. This is
the promise of the Lord for you – in a world that is full of
danger, you and your family are safe!

Parent Declaration:

No evil can come near my children today. They have
supernatural protection everywhere they go, for God's angels

are with them. He has commanded them to do nothing today but watch over my children, holding them up and keeping them safe. No sickness can come near our household, and no plan of the enemy can prosper against us.

Kid Declaration:

No evil can come near me today – my angels are keeping me safe!

Resource: Here are 10 Bible verses about protection

DAY FOURTEEN

Correction Brings Wisdom

"Foolishness is bound up in the heart of a child; the rod of correction will drive it far from him...The rod and rebuke give wisdom, but a child left to himself brings shame to his mother."

Proverbs 22:15, 29:15

Today's Meditation:

We were all born into this world with foolishness bound in our hearts. It's not a reflection on you as a parent – it's a reflection of the sin nature we're all born with. If left unattended, foolishness *stays* in a child's heart, and they grow up to be a fool (do a study of "fool" in the book of Proverbs – it's not something we want to be!). But thankfully, the Bible says there's a way to remove this foolishness – that is with the rod of correction. Not the rod of punishment or cruelty, but correction. As we see in the verse above, the rod of correction gives a child wisdom (do a study of wisdom too – you'll like it!). Wisdom is much preferable to foolishness.

Parent Declaration:

Father, help me to consistently and lovingly correct my children so that foolishness does not guide their life. I believe Your Word, and I will apply it diligently. I declare that each time I correct them the way the Bible instructs me to, Your promise is working, and foolishness is removed. Thank You that these boundaries formed in their childhood will help them live disciplined, happy lives.

Kid Declaration:

Foolishness is removed from my heart when my parents correct me. The rod gives me wisdom.

Resource: For more about the right way to apply correction, check out my Parenting With a Purpose materials.

DAY FIFTEEN

Enjoy the Teenage Years

"Train up a child in the way he should go, and when he is older he will not depart from it."

Proverbs 22:6

Today's Meditation:

One of the great benefits of training your child according to the Bible is that it can make the teenage years harmonious. Not perfect, mind you, but not horrible either. Contrary to what the world says, teenagers are not trying to drive parents crazy – they're trying to grow up! They're just not very good at it yet. Around age 9 or so, they begin the separation process. If you have instilled biblical principles in their hearts, their teenage years can be *fun!* Remember that everything is changing in their world, and more than anything else, they want your respect. So be their biggest cheerleader. Be available to talk. Let them make some mistakes, then help them get back on track. Stop speaking to them in commands, and ask them (often) the most important question a parent can ask a teenager: "What do *you* think?" Then listen to them.

Parent Declaration:

Father, I declare that my child's teenage years will be *fun!* I will be their biggest cheerleader, and let them know I'm always on their side. I will often ask their opinion, and I will listen respectfully to their ideas. I will let them make their own mistakes and guide them back on track. Thank You for helping me to walk through their teenage years with joy and peace and faith.

Kid Declaration:

I've been trained by the Word of God, and I'll never stop living by it.

Resource: For more help, read my blog "5 Tips for Growing a Teenager."

DAY SIXTEEN

Our Family's Gift to the World

"Like arrows in the hand of a warrior, so are the children of one's youth. Happy is the man who has his quiver full of them; they shall not be ashamed, but shall speak with their enemies in the gate."

Psalm 127:4, 5

Today's Meditation:

According to this verse, your child is like an arrow—a weapon! And arrows are not meant to be kept in the quiver. God wants you eventually to *shoot* them out into the world to make an impact with the love of Christ. Your children are your gift to the world. The reason you're so happy with a full quiver is because your children will grow up to be a help and a blessing to *you*. In Bible times the city gate was the place where justice was administered and the citizens met for business or social intercourse. A parent with stalwart and influential children would run no risk of being wronged by enemies. Raising strong children into a strong family is a blessing to both them and you!

Parent Declaration:

My children are a gift from God to this household, and our family's gift to the world. They are like arrows in my hand, shot out into the world to impact people with the love of Christ, and to bring me blessing, victory and honor. They have a divine destiny; I will point them toward the bullseye, toward an intimate relationship with Jesus, so they can fulfill it.

Kid Declaration:

I am like an arrow, being shot out into the world to honor my family and make an impact with the love of Christ.

Resource: *Read more about how to craft your arrow here:* http://goo.gl/7CWwYw.

DAY SEVENTEEN

Be Increase-minded

"The Lord shall increase you more and more, you and your children."

Psalms 115:14

Today's Meditation:

I love this verse! After my first husband died when our boys were 12 and 13, I declared this verse over us *a lot* and I can testify that it has come to pass in our lives. We have increased not only financially, but also in every area of our lives. No matter what it looks like in your world today, begin to say what God says about you. It says He *shall* increase you and your children, not He *might*. Mark 11:23 says you can have whatever you say. Begin to declare this wonderful truth today, and watch God begin to perform His Word on your behalf!

Parent Declaration:

I declare that the increase of the Lord is being poured out on our family, and my children are not left out! We are increasing more and more! More wisdom, more joy, more peace, more financial abundance, more health – more of everything Jesus died to give us – is being poured out on my children and our family today.

Kid Declaration:

The Lord is increasing my family and me, more and more every day!

Resource: For more about increase read my blog "The Day I Learned I was Rich"

DAY EIGHTEEN

Send Them Out into the World

"[Father] I do not pray that You should take them out of the world, but that You should keep them from the evil one. They are not of the world, just as I am not of the world. Sanctify them by Your truth. Your word is truth. As You sent Me into the world, I also have sent them into the world."

John 17:15-18

Today's Meditation:

The verse above is the prayer that Jesus prayed over His disciples. As parents, many times we want to shield our children from the world and all its troubles – but like the disciples, in the right time, there is a work for them to do in this world. The Christian life isn't freedom from work, but strength to do it; not freedom from temptation, but power to overcome it; not living apart from the world, but living holy lives that leaven it. And we can trust God to keep them safe from the evil one, and to sanctify them by His Word as they serve Him.

Parent Declaration:

Father, I do not ask that You take my children out of the world, but that You keep and protect them from the evil one. They are not worldly (belonging to the world), just as I am not of the world. Sanctify them by the truth of Your Word - purify, consecrate, separate them for Yourself, make them holy. Just as You sent me into the world, I also send them into the world.

Kid Declaration:

I am not worldly, and I'm protected from the evil one as I go out into the world to tell people about Jesus.

DAY NINETEEN

Be Kind and Forgive

"Stop being mean, bad-tempered, and angry. Quarreling, harsh words, and dislike of others should have no place in your lives. Instead, be kind to each other, tenderhearted, forgiving one another, just as God has forgiven you because you belong to Christ."

Ephesians 4:31, 32 (TLB)

Today's Meditation:

This is a good verse for all of us to put into practice everywhere, every day. But we should especially practice it daily in our family! Somehow, we are rudest or most thoughtless to the people closest to us – that shouldn't be so. Let's make an effort to speak words of blessing and edification over our children today. Let's admit when we're wrong, which is one way to train our kids to forgive. We can determine today to set the tone for kindness and forgiveness in our home.

Parent Declaration:

With the help of the Holy Spirit, today I speak words over my children that bless and edify them. We don't hold grudges in our family – we forgive. I teach them to say, "I'm sorry" by saying it myself when I'm wrong. We are kind to one another, respecting each other and treating each other with the love of Christ.

Kid Declaration:

I won't be mean or mad today. I'll be kind and forgive everyone because Jesus forgave me.

Resource: *For help admitting you're wrong (!) read my blog* "Saying You're Sorry"

DAY TWENTY

Living By the Word

"You shall love the LORD your God with all your heart, with all your soul, and with all your strength. And these words which I command you today shall be in your heart. You shall teach them diligently to your children, and shall talk of them when you sit in your house, when you walk by the way, when you lie down, and when you rise up. You shall bind them as a sign on your hand, and they shall be as frontlets between your eyes. You shall write them on the doorposts of your house and on your gates."

Deut. 6:5-9

Today's Meditation:

Today's verse shows us that we aren't to just read God's Word once a day and then forget it – we're supposed to live by it. Keep it in our hearts and minds. Teach it diligently to our kids. Talk about it at the house and when we're out; when we go to bed and when we get up. In other words, when things happen, we should go to the "manual for life" (the Bible) first to see how we should think and conduct ourselves. We should always bring it into our conversations, and let it be our final authority. Let your children know that when we live by the Word, we're living in line with God's perfect will!

Parent Declaration:

Father, help me to diligently teach Your Word to my children every day, not just in church. Let Your Word be a way of life in our household. We will talk of You and recount Your wonderful deeds all day long. We will read Your stories and listen to Your voice, and my children will not just know *about* You, but they will *know* You as the Most High God.

Kid Declaration:

I love to read the Bible – I'll act the way it says to, and do what it tells me to do.

DAY TWENTY ONE

Praying For Their Future Spouse

"Wives, submit to your own husbands, as to the Lord…Husbands, love your wives, just as Christ also loved the church and gave Himself for her…"

Ephesians 5:22, 25

Today's Meditation:

Getting married is one of life's biggest events, and who your child marries makes a huge difference in the direction of their life. No matter how old your child is right now, why not start believing for their mate ahead of time? I prayed for my daughters-in-love from the time my sons were very small, and I can tell you – it was worth it! They are two of the most delightful, smart, loving, God-serving women I know, and I'm so blessed to have them in our family! Now's the time to start speaking over your child's prospective mate.

Parent Declaration:

Father, I thank You that You are preparing the perfect mate for my child, who will help them follow God all the days of their life. My child will marry someone who loves and believes You and wants to serve You – they will not be unequally yoked. Their spouse is being perfected in love and developing in the fruit of the Spirit. They are each learning the lessons now that will help them have a marriage that is "heaven on earth."

Kid Declaration:

When I grow up, I will marry someone who loves God and helps me follow Him.

DAY TWENTY TWO

Good Friend, Good Spouse

"Greater love has no one than this, that one lay down his life for his friends."

John 15:13 (NASB)

Today's Meditation:

The world's idea of how to choose a spouse is very skewed, and really offers no foundation for a lasting, loving marriage. I believe the best way we can train our children to recognize a good candidate for marriage, and also how to *be* a good spouse, is to train them to be a good *friend* as they grow up. Think about it -- the qualities of a good spouse are the same as those of a good friend: they are faithful, they are for you, they cry when you cry and are joyous over your victories, they stand up for you, they tell you the truth, what's theirs is yours, etc. Let's seek to help our children nurture these qualities in their current friendships, so they can recognize counterfeits.

Parent Declaration:

Father, help my child recognize good relationships in their life. Arrange times where we can talk about the good qualities we look for in friends, and give us teachable moments where we can talk about their own behavior toward their true friends. Bring good friends into my child's life – those who will influence them positively in every way: spiritually, emotionally, mentally, and physically. Help my child be a faithful, truthful, loving and sharing friend, so they can be a faithful, truthful, loving and sharing spouse when they grow up.

Kid Declaration:

God, bring me good friends, and help me be a good friend to them too.

DAY TWENTY THREE

God's Top Priority

"...the love of God has been poured out in our hearts by the Holy Spirit who was given to us."

Romans 5:5

Today's Meditation:

The Gospel can be described in one word: **love**. God loved us so much He sent His only Son to deliver us from sin (John 3:16). Jesus gave us *one* commandment to follow: love one another (John 15:12). He said that *this* (walking in love) would be how people recognize that we are Christians. Of all the things we teach our children, love is at the top of God's priority list. Begin today to speak this amazing, life-changing agape love over your children, and make walking in love a priority in your family.

Parent Declaration:

I speak the love of God over my children, and I call for that love which is in them to rise up every day. I walk in love with my children, and they walk in love with me and everyone else they meet. This perfect love in our hearts never fails (1 Cor. 13:8) and casts out all fear in our lives (1 John 4:18).

Kid Declaration:

God's perfect love is inside me, so I am not afraid and I can love people today.

Resource: *To receive a greater understanding of God's love check out my* CD *or* MP3 *"God Loves You."*

DAY TWENTY FOUR

A Work in Progress

"...it is God who works in you both to will and to do for His good pleasure."

Philippians 2:13

Today's Meditation:

Sometimes our children show no sign of acting wisely! I know you know what I mean. But here's the deal -- they're still a work in progress (and really, aren't we all?). Now is the time to keep them surrounded with your faith, especially if they're acting unwisely! God has promised that He's working in them. Aren't you glad? It's not *you* working in them, and it's not *them* working in them – it's God! He knows how to grow them up as we surround them with our faith. So let's continue to speak and believe wisdom over our children today, no matter what we see.

Parent Declaration:

Father, I ask that You give my children liberal wisdom as You promised to in James 1:5. I declare that they have the wisdom of God in all matters of life — at school, at home, at work, and with their peers. They are a work in progress, and I will continue to believe that You are working in them! I speak what I *want* over them and what Your Word says, not what I *see*.

Kid Declaration:

God is working in me so that I grow up pleasing Him!

DAY TWENTY FIVE

Think About What You're Thinking About

"The thoughts of the righteous are right… For as he thinks in his heart, so is he…bringing every thought into captivity to the obedience of Christ…."

Proverbs 12:5,23:7, 2 Cor 10:5

Today's Meditation:

It's amazing to realize that everything in our life, good or bad, starts with our thoughts. Nobody sins without thinking about it first. Strongholds (lies from the devil) come from our thoughts. Ulcers, headaches and a myriad of other health issues can be caused by dwelling on negative thoughts. Even stress comes from what we're thinking about. We can't think one thing and *believe* another. We can't think about how sick we are and believe we're healed. We can't dwell on our mistakes or inabilities and move forward in faith. So our thoughts are vitally important! Let's speak words of faith over our children today regarding their thoughts.

Parent Declaration:

Father, help me and my children to think right thoughts today – thoughts that are in line with who we are as the righteousness of God in Christ. Help us to instantly recognize thoughts from the enemy so we can bring every thought captive to the obedience of Christ, in line with Your Word. I declare that our family is winning the battlefield of the mind today – we think thoughts that are edifying, true, uplifting, God-pleasing, empowering, and right, in Jesus' Name.

Kid Declaration:

I'll be careful what I'm thinking about today, and only think thoughts that please God!

Resource: For more help with thoughts, check out my video "What Was I Thinking?"

DAY TWENTY SIX

Obedience Brings Blessing

"Children, obey your parents in the Lord, for this is right. Honor your father and mother—which is the first commandment with a promise— so that it may go well with you and that you may enjoy long life on the earth."

Ephesians 6:1

Today's Meditation:

According to the Bible, children have just *one* commandment upon their lives – to obey their parents. (God knew they had a short attention span, so He only gave them one!). So that means as parents, our goal in teaching our children to obey us isn't to make us look good, or even for us to have peace in our lives – it's to help them fulfill God's one commandment upon their life. Since we love our children – we want things to go well with them and for them to enjoy long life – then it's our job to diligently and consistently train them to obey us. It's not an option, and it's not just for sometimes. It's for their benefit and blessing!

Parent Declaration:

I will diligently and consistently help my child learn to obey me -- first time, every time -- because I love them. I want things to go well with them and I want them to enjoy long life on the earth, so it's my responsibility to help them learn obedience. I will teach them this verse and the other verses in this book, so they understand God's will for them and how to receive His blessings in their life. I will help them to understand that obedience brings blessing, and disobedience brings trouble. I declare that I have obedient children, in Jesus' Name.

Kid Declaration:

I will obey my parents today so things can go well with me, and I can enjoy a long life!

Resource: *For more about teaching your child obedience, check out my series* "Parenting With a Purpose."

DAY TWENTY SEVEN

Raising God's Last Days Army

"And it shall come to pass afterward, that I will pour out my spirit upon all flesh; and your sons and daughters shall prophesy, your old men shall dream dreams, your young men shall see visions: And also upon your servants and upon the handmaidens in those days I will pour out my spirit."

Joel 2:28

Today's Meditation:

Sometimes it's easy, in the midst of our everyday lives, to get focused on the tyranny of the urgent and to forget the real purpose of our lives as Christians. We are here to proclaim Jesus! To raise up our children in the loving discipline of the Lord (Eph. 6:4 MSG) so they can fulfill *their* divine destiny and *His* divine purpose on the earth. When we keep that big-picture perspective, it makes every day an adventure in God, and keeps our everyday problems in their proper place. It helps us to focus more on training, encouraging, and undergirding our children to do what God has called them to do – because they're anointed to do it!

Parent Declaration:

My children are anointed by the Spirit of God to be bold witnesses in these last days. We are raising up God's last days army! Years and years ago, God made a promise to this generation, and we know that He is pouring out His Spirit upon them. They prophesy, dream spiritual dreams and see heaven-sent visions. They are sensitive to the Holy Spirit. They have the heart of a servant, to serve the Lord with their whole life.

Kid Declaration:

God has poured His Spirit out on me so I can fulfill my divine destiny!

DAY TWENTY EIGHT

Living Well For the Master

"...asking God to give you wise minds and spirits attuned to his will, and so acquire a thorough understanding of the ways in which God works. We pray that you'll live well for the Master, making him proud of you as you work hard in his orchard. As you learn more and more how God works, you will learn how to do your work."

Colossians 1:9, 10 (MSG)

Today's Meditation:

I think it's the desire of every Christian parent that their child grows up wise with spirits that are attuned to God. I'm sure you're like me and you want your child to live well for the Master! That happens as they learn more about how God works, who He is, and how He looks at us. And we all learn that by spending time in His Word. The Bible is our manual for life, it's how we know what to expect from God. As we make family Bible time a priority in our homes, we're giving our children a wonderful foundation for wisdom.

Parent Declaration:

My children are filled with the knowledge of God's will, and they have spiritual understanding. Every day they understand more of His ways. Father, help them to walk worthy of You and please You in everything they do. I call them fruitful in everything they do, and increasing in the knowledge of You, understanding how You work and what You expect from them. Lead and guide them every step of the way today.

Kid Declaration:

I want to live well for the Master today, and please Him in everything I do!

DAY TWENTY NINE

The Blood of Jesus

"And they overcame him by the blood of the Lamb, and by the word of their testimony…"

Revelation 12:11

Today's Meditation:

The blood of Jesus is what seals the deal of our covenant with God, making it unbreakable. Our covenant is not based on something perishable like silver or gold, but upon the *most* precious thing in the universe, the blood of God's only son (1 Peter 1:18). Jesus' blood is what paid the price for our sin, the price we could never pay (1 John 1:7); it's the proof that we are reconciled to God (Colossians 1:20) and it has healed us (1 Peter 2:24). Blood is the sign that God used as His protection for His people (Exodus 12:7). Let's use the power of the blood over our children today.

Parent Declaration:

In the name of Jesus, I plead the blood over my children today. They are protected, saved, sanctified, and healed by that blood. They have a bloodline of protection around them, keeping the light in and the darkness out of their lives – the devil has no right to cross that line. My children are overcomers. They overcome the flesh, the world and the devil because of the precious blood of Jesus, and because they testify of His salvation.

Kid Declaration:

The blood of Jesus is the proof of my covenant with God. By the blood I am saved, protected and healed!

Resource: *For more about your blood covenant, check out my* CD *or MP3 "Your Covenant With God."*

DAY THIRTY

Refuse to Worry

"Be anxious for nothing, but in everything by prayer and supplication, with thanksgiving, let your requests be made known to God; and the peace of God, which surpasses all understanding, will guard your hearts and minds through Christ Jesus."

Philippians 4:6,7

Today's Meditation:

In these verses God instructs us to not worry or be anxious about *anything!* That sounds almost impossible for a parent, but thankfully He tells us how to do it. When we're tempted to worry, He tells us to *pray about it*. One version says, "Tell God what you need." Simple enough, huh? So pray first, before you do anything else! And then don't forget to thank Him. Thank Him for hearing and answering (it's hard to be thankful and worried at the same time – thanking Him is like saying, "I trust You Lord, I believe You're working on it"). When we refuse to worry and we pray, this scripture promises us that God's peace will descend upon us. The first part is up to us – the second part is up to Him. He can't give us the peace until we give Him the problem and refuse to worry.

Parent Declaration:

I will not fret, worry, or have any anxiety over anything concerning my children. I bring every concern and care to God in prayer, and He takes care of it with tender loving care. He floods my heart and mind, and my children's hearts and minds, with peace that passes understanding.

Kid Declaration:

I'm not going to worry about anything today. Father God, thank You for taking care of everything!

Resource: *For more help resisting worry, check out my* CD *or* MP3 *"Don't Worry."*

DAY THIRTY ONE

When They're Hurting

"The Spirit of the Lord is upon me, because He has anointed me…to heal the brokenhearted."

Luke 4:18

Today's Meditation:

There are things that happen in a child's life that can wound their soul – disappointments, fearful events, harsh words, teasing or bullying, tragedies, etc. We like to protect our children from these things as much as possible, but sometimes they do happen. Thankfully, Jesus knows that, and He has promised to heal their heart and restore their soul (Psalm 23:3). He's the only one who can. As parents we can surround a wounded child with faith and believe these verses above, so they won't carry those wounds into tomorrow.

Parent Declaration:

Father, I know that You've been to my child's future and back and You knew there would be bumps along the road of their life. You knew their hearts might be wounded, and I thank You that you've already made provision to heal them! Thank You for ministering life to their heart, healing every hurt, and restoring their mind, will, and emotions – You are the only one who can. I trust You to do it!

Kid Declaration:

Jesus loves me so much! He heals my heart and restores my soul.

TO CONNECT WITH

Karen Jensen Salisbury

VISIT KARENSALISBURY.ORG

- BLOG
- ITINERARY
- CONTACT
- RESOURCES

Made in the USA
Middletown, DE
29 April 2017